Venice 8

Enrico Massetti

Copyright Enrico Massetti 2016

Published by Enrico Massetti

All Rights Reserved

Third edition

Venice

Canal Grande

We will make no attempt to rehearse the glorious history or list the countless treasures of this unique city. We will merely outline a tour in which we have attempted the difficult undertaking of offering the visitor the best of Venice in two days. The itinerary can be extended by spending more time in the museums while following the same layout. You can also add a day in the Lagoon Islands and more days in the nearby cities of Verona, Vicenza or Padua..

To try and mention all the streets would be impossible; the various stages of our tour will serve as reference points instead of asking the helpful and patient Venetians for the right direction. Don't be depressed if you lose the way: it happens to them, too.

This is the itinerary to follow if you actually have at least two full days in Venice. I say that because many of you will be arriving in Venice by plane or by train, in which case—sad to say—on that first day you don't actually have a full day to spend here, since much of the morning will be spent traveling and finding your hotel.

If you arrive in Venice late in the day, try taking a Grand Canal cruise on the *Vaporetto* ending in St. Mark's Square. These sights are more romantic and much less crowded after dark—and they provide a wonderful welcome to the city.

Venice is small. You can walk across it, from head to tail, in about an hour. Nearly all of your sightseeing is within a 20-minute walk of the Rialto Bridge or St.

Mark's Square. Remember that Venice itself is its greatest sight. When you cross the bridge, following your itinerary, look both ways: you may be hit with a lovely view.

St. Mark Square

Piazza San Marco

We start early in the morning from Piazza San Marco, the most beautiful drawing room in Europe, according to Napoleon, to avoid the midday crowds around St. Mark's Basilica and the Doge's Palace. Generations of artists and artisans have given it the appearance we now know, through ten centuries of uninterrupted labour; so that today the square in its entirety strikes us as a single complex work, a masterpiece of Italian taste and imagination.

Saint Mark's Basilica

San Mark Cathedral

In front of us is the Basilica di San Marco, founded in 828 and embellished uninterruptedly until the end of the 16th century. Greek and medieval, Byzantine and Tuscan, Lombard and Venetian art have contributed to its decoration, in every possible medium of expression, from mosaics to the work of goldsmiths, from sculpture to painting.

Opening hours:

Basilica: 9.45 a.m. - 5.00 p.m. - *Sunday and holidays:* 2.00 p.m. - 4.00 p.m. (entrance free)

St. Mark's Museum: 9.45 a.m. - 4.45 p.m. (entrance: 5 €)
Pala d'oro: 9.45 a.m. - 4.00 p.m. - *Sunday and holidays:* 2.00 p.m. - 4.00 p.m. (entrance: 2 €)
Treasury: 9.45 a.m. - 4.00 p.m. - *Sunday and holidays:* 2.00 p.m. - 4.00 p.m. (entrance: 3 €)

St Mark's Basilica

The Basilica is a wonderful example of Byzantine Venetian architecture. It was at one time the Doge's chapel but it was also the mausoleum for Saint Mark, the patron saint, whose life is narrated in the golden mosaics on the walls.

With five cupolas, it was built (10th century) to house the body of the St Mark the Evangelist.

The facade features five portals decorated in splendid marbles and mosaics, and with a terrace dividing it into two halves.

Saint Mark's horses

Four Horses

On the terrace stand Four Horses of gilded copper (copies – the originals are now preserved inside) that were sent from Constantinople to Doge Enrico Dandolo in 1204.

Splendid mosaics in the atrium relate the stories of the Bible.

The imposing interior in the form of a Greek cross contains a wealth of paintings and sculptures.

Saint Mark's Basilica interior

St Mark's interior

Of particular interest are mosaics of Venetian-Byzantine origin, some of them reconstructed from drawings by Titian, Tintoretto and Veronese.

The Bell Tower adjacent to the basilica was once a lighthouse for ships. At the foot of the tower is a 16th century loggia by J. Sansovino.

Doge's Palace

Doge's Palace

To the right of the Basilica, we go through the Porta delta Carta and into the Doge's Palace, built in the florid Gothic style typical of Venice (1303-1442). The Renaissance courtyard was designed by Antonio Rizzo (1483), who also left the two masterpieces of Venetian sculpture there, the statues of Adam and Eve (1464), now in the Doge's Apartments.

Going up the Scala dei Giganti, we enter the incredibly lavish interior of the palace. It features carved and gilded ceilings, stuccoes, fireplaces and carved doors. It is one of the most gorgeous public residences of all times. Venetian painters, from Carpaccio to Gentile Bellini, from Titian to Veronese, and to Bassano, have created fantastic allegories, in which the glory of Venice, both in fact and in legend, is the dominating theme. We will be astonished by the gigantic canvas of Paradise by Tintoretto, the largest in existence.

Tiepolo: *Neptune Offering Gifts to Venice*

Marvelous paintings hang on the walls, including the sublime Piety by Giovanni Bellini and three rare works by Hieronymus Bosch: Paradise, Hell and the Martyrdom of St. Juliana.

Opening hours of the Doge's Palace

from April 1st to October 31st
8.30 am – 7 pm (last admission 6 pm)

from November 1st to March 31st
8.30 am – 5.30 pm (last admission 4.30 pm)

The Piazzetta

Lion of St. Mark column

Leaving the Palace, we go and stand on the side of the Piazzetta facing the Lagoon; on top of the two columns (12th century), are statues of St. Theodore and of the Lion of St. Mark. Before our eyes, we have the light-filled panorama of St. Mark's Dock, at one time crowded with the fleet of the Republic.

The view is dominated by the Island of San Giorgio Maggiore: then to the left is the Lido, and the Riva degli Schiavoni; to the right, the Giudecca and the Customs-House Point and nearby the Basilica della Salute.

Procuratie Vecchie

Procuratie Vecchie at right

Opposite the Ducal Palace, stands the Libreria Vecchia, seat of the National Marciana Library, designed by Sansovino. Also by Sansovino is the stupendous Loggetta (1540) along the base of the Campanile. Extending down the two longer sides of the square are the Procuratie (ancient offices of the Venetian State). Next to the Procuratie Vecchie (1532) is the Clock Tower (1496) with its famous clock-work figures of the Moors.

Fabbrica Nueva

Procuratie Nuove at Carnival

The last section of the square, opposite St. Mark's, is known as the Fabbrica Nueva, or the Napoleonic ring, since it was built at the orders of Napoleon. Under the arcade of this side, we enter the Correr Museum, an important collection relating to civil and maritime history, of Venetian costumes and mementos, and magnificent paintings, including the Pieta by Antonello da Messina, the Trasfigurazione by Giovanni Bellini, and the Courtesans by Carpaccio.

Basilica della Salute

Basilica della Salute

Leaving the square and passing the Baroque church of San Moise, we reach Santa Maria del Giglio, then take the nearby ferry and cross the Grand Canal to the Customs-House Point where, a few steps away, we come to the basilica della Salute, an architectural masterpiece of Baldassare Longhena (1631-1687). Inside, there are magnificent paintings by Titian, Tintoretto, Luca Giordano.

Riva delle Zattere

Zattere at Gesuati

Passing over a small bridge we come to the fine Gothic Abbey of San Gregorio, closed at present. Following the little canal, we reach the spacious Riva delle Zattere, across from the Giudecca.

Passing beyond the Lombard Church of the Holy Spirit, and going along the quayside by the red walls and gardens, we reach the Church of the Gesuati, which contains one of Tiepolo's finest canvases (Madonna and S. Caterina).

Church of the Gesuati

Gian Battista Tiepolo

The order of the Gesuati was suppressed in 1868 and the church and monastery were handed over to the Dominicans. In 1724 the architect Giorgio Massari was commissioned to build the new church. The inside has no side naves but contains altar pieces by Piazzetta, Sebastiano Ricci and Gian Battista Tiepolo.

The latter was also commissioned with decorating the ceiling with illustrations of the history of the Dominicans. The Gesuati church was rebuilt in 1657 on the site of a former church of the Crucifix Order.

The façade was paid for by the Manins and built by Fattoretto featuring baroque architecture with a very plastic character.

Accademia

Accademia Gallery

From here, we take the narrow, tree-lined street next to the church to the former church of the Carita on the Grand Canal. Today, this Gothic church forms part of the Accademia Galleries, the most important collection of paintings in Venice, the entrance to which is next door.

The **Gallerie dell'Accademia** is a museum gallery of pre-19th-century art. It is housed in the Scuola della Carità on the south bank of the Grand Canal, within the sestiere of Dorsoduro. It was originally the gallery of the Accademia di Belle Arti di Venezia, the art academy of Venice, from which it became independent in 1879, and for which the Ponte dell'Accademia and the Accademia boat landing station for the *vaporetto* water bus are named. The two institutions remained in the same building until 2004, when the art school moved to the Ospedale degli Incurabili.

Leonardo da Vinci's Vitruvian man

Artists represented include: Lazzaro Bastiani, Gentile and Giovanni Bellini, Bernardo Bellotto, Pacino di Bonaguida, Canaletto, Carpaccio, Giulio Carpioni, Rosalba Carriera, Cima da Conegliano, Fetti, Pietro Gaspari, Michele Giambono, Luca Giordano, Francesco Guardi, Giorgione, Johann Liss, Charles Le Brun, Pietro Longhi, Lorenzo Lotto, Mantegna, Rocco Marconi, Michele Marieschi, Antonello da Messina, Piazzetta, Giambattista Pittoni, Preti, Tiepolo, Tintoretto, Titian, Veronese (Paolo Caliari), Vasari, Leonardo da Vinci (Drawing of Vitruvian Man), Alvise Vivarini, and Giuseppe Zais.

Ca' Rezzonico

Ca' Rezzonico

Leaving the Accademia, we go through the maze of narrow streets which take us to the 18th century church of S. Barnaba, and lead to Ca' Rezzonico, an imposing building designed by Longhena which houses paintings, marvelous furniture, costumes, ceramics, books, etc.

The palace was adapted to serve as the museum and opened to the public on April 25th 1936. The designers of the museum layout, Nino Barbantini and Giulio Lorenzetti, aimed to exploit the character of Ca' Rezzonico, arranging the works as if they were the palace's original furnishings. To achieve this result, numerous 18th century works that belonged to the other museums of Venice were moved to Ca' Rezzonico, together with paintings, furniture, and frescoes from other civic-owned buildings and many works purchased for the occasion.

The final effect was undeniably striking; the quality of the numerous works exhibited, together with the extraordinary quality of the architecture and the setting, made Ca' Rezzonico a veritable temple of the Venetian 18th century: an age of splendor, dissipation, and decadence, but undoubtedly one of the most lively and fertile seasons of modern art in Europe.

Scuola Grande di San Rocco (Confraternity)

Paintings in the sala superiore - Scuola Grande di San Rocco

Passing behind Palazzo Foscari, beyond the Rio Nuovo and the quaint Campo di S. Margherita, we come to the Church and School (1508-1530) of San Rocco. In the Great Hall of the School, Jacopo Tintoretto has left an incredible cycle of paintings (21 on the ceiling and 13 on the walls) which constitutes his masterpiece.

Located in the campo bearing the same name. In 1478, it was made into a charitable institution. The present building was started in 1489 and finished in the sixteenth century by the architect Giangiacomo dei Grigi. It is famous for displaying a series of paintings by Tintoretto that adorn the rooms. Next to the school there is the church, which is also dedicated to San Rocco. It was built in the sixteenth century and was renovated by Giovanni Scalfurotto in the eighteenth century. Built in the first half of the 16th C, the Guildhall of San Rocco is the home of an extraordinary cycle of canvases by J. Tintoretto, among which eight on the ground floor portray Scenes from the New Testament.

Tintoretto dedicated scenes taken from the Old Testament to the ceiling of the Upper Hall, while on the walls the cycle of paintings includes the great painter's self-portrait.

Church of the Frari (Santa Maria Gloriosa dei Frari)

Santa Maria Gloriosa dei Frari - interior

From here, we go to Santa Maria Gloriosa dei Frari, a solemn Gothic church whose interior is dominated by the luminous canvas of Our Lady of the Assumption by Titian (1518). Other paintings (Titian Bellini, etc.) and the numerous sculptures by great Venetian artists lend this church all the importance of a museum.

It was built in the fourteenth century by the Franciscans, who settled in Venice from about 1222. Rebuilt in the fifteenth century, it bears witness to the Venetian Republic with paintings by Titian and Bellini. It is an example of Gothic architecture from the middle of the fifteenth century, and has one of the highest bell towers in Venice, which was started in 1361.

Once known as Ca' Grande, erected between 1236 and 1338 through the efforts of the Conventual Franciscan Friars Minor, it was replaced by a grandiose Gothic Franciscan-style edifice in the 14th century, with a nave and two aisles and seven apsidal chapels.

The imposing 14th century brick bell tower is one of the highest in Venice. The Basilica is one of the most important sacred buildings owing to the wealth of artworks that it houses. The interior, in the Latin cross plan, features precious paintings such as one of the masterpieces of Titian's mature work, the Altarpiece of the Assumption (1516-1518), intended by the artist for the high altar.

Other works worthy of note are the Triptych of the Virgin and Saints by Giovanni Bellini (1488), located in the Pesaro Chapel of the Sacresty and considered to be one of the masterpieces of 15th century Venetian art, and the wooden statue of St John the Baptist, a superb work by Donatello.

Campo San Polo

Campo San Polo

A short walk brings us to the lively Campo San Polo, with its beautiful palaces, and if we continue parallel to the Grand Canal, which can be seen glinting at the ends of the various smaller canals, we reach the ancient little church of S. Giacomo a Rialto, with its large clock and its remarkable bell-tower, standing in the midst of the bustling market place.

Rialto Bridge

Rialto Bridge

Passing over the famous Rialto Bridge (1591), with its beautiful view of the Grand Canal, we reach Campo San Bartolomeo, and then turn right to the church of San Salvatore, the facade of which was designed by Sansovino and Scamozzi (inside, there is the Annunciation and Transfiguration by Titian).

Palazzo Contarini (called Del Bovolo)

Palazzo Contarini (called Del Bovolo)

Anybody can tell you the way to the 15th century Palazzo Contarini (called Del Bovolo), with its ingenious spiral staircase, and from there we can make our way to the elegant Campo Santo Stefano. with its austere 14th century church (paintings by B. Vivarini, Carpaccio, Piazzetta, Tintoretto).

Teatro della Fenice

Teatro della Fenice - interior

We can sit down in one of the cafes on the Campo to rest, before returning to Piazza San Marco by way of the Teatro della Fenice.

The Theater is one of the most famous and renowned landmarks in the history of Italian theatre as well as those in Europe. Especially in the 19th century, La Fenice became the site of many famous operatic premieres at which the works of several of the four major *bel canto* era composers—Rossini, Bellini, Donizetti, and Verdi were performed.

Its name reflects its role in permitting an opera company to "*rise from the ashes*" despite losing the use of three theaters to fire, the first in 1774 after the city's leading house was destroyed and rebuilt but not opened until 1792; the second fire came in 1836, but rebuilding was completed within a year. However, the third fire was the result of arson. It destroyed the house in 1996 leaving only the exterior walls, but it was rebuilt and re-opened in November 2004.

If we still have the strength (by now it should be evening according to our schedule), we can walk down the Mercerie and admire its lovely shops.

Second day

Bridge of Sighs

The next day we set off from Piazza San Marco in the opposite direction. Passing by the Bridge of Sighs, with its romantic associations, and the adjoining Prison, we turn inland towards the church of San Zaccaria, a masterpiece of Venetian Renaissance architecture, designed by Coducci (1500). Inside, a famous Madonna by Giovanni Bellini, works by Tintoretto and in the gem-like chapel of S. Tarasio, polyptychs by Vivarini, Giovanni D'Alemagna and frescoes by the Florentine painter Andrea del Castagno may be seen.

From San Zaccaria, we go to the little church of S. Maria Formosa, in the square (campo) of the same name (featuring an important Triptych by B. Vivarini, and S. Barnaba by Palma il Vecchio). In the same square, too, is the Querini Stampalia Gallery, with an outstanding collection of Venetian paintings, especially from the 18th century, with the wonderful series of scenes of domestic and street life, painted by Pietro Longhi. We come to Palazzo Prili, an extremely fine Venetian-Gothic building, and soon reach one of the sanctuaries of Venetian painting: the School of San Giorgio degli Schiavoni, containing the striking History of St. George, a series of pictures painted by Vittorio Carpaccio between 1501 and 1511.

S. Francesco della Vigna

S. Francesco della Vigna

We then come to the Palladian church of S. Francesco della Vigna (1572) with a delightful cloister (inside, a rare Madonna by Antonio da Negioponte, 1450, and paintings by Bellini, Vivarini, and Veronese; an important Lombard marble triptych in the Giustiniani Chapel), and then the vast Campo (square) which takes its name from the Church of San Giovanni e Paolo (1246-1430) the Pantheon of Venetian glories, with its severe aisled nave, paintings by Bellini and frescoes by Piazzetta as well as the magnificent tombs of illustrious Venetians. In the middle of the square, the vigorous statue of the famous Italian soldier of fortune, Bartolommeo Colleoni, executed by Andrea Verrocchio (1488) the teacher of Leonardo da Vinci. We suggest making a detour at this point to go and admire the flawless lines of S. Maria act Miracoli, designed by Pietro Lombardo (1489).

Returning to S. Giovanni e Paolo, we walk along the quaint Rio dei Mendicanti to the Fondamenta Nuove, and then along the side of the lagoon as far as the 18th century Church of the Jesuits, standing in a peaceful square of the same name. From here, we return to the Grand Canal to enjoy a veritable gem of Venetian Gothic architecture, the Ca' d'Oro (1421-1440) which contains the second most important picture gallery in Venice (the dramatic S. Sebastiano by Mantegna, a Venus by Titian, works by Vivarini, Carpaccio, Lippi, Ghirlandaio, Signorelli, etc.).

Campo dell'Abazia

Campo dell'Abazia

We now make for the solitary Gothic Church of the Misericordia and next to the School of the same name: this is one of the most picturesque spots in Venice, at the point where two canals are crossed by an attractive wooden bridge. We then carry on to the Church of the Madonna dell'Orto, where Tintoretto, who lived nearby and who is buried in the church, left another remarkable series of paintings. Returning to the Grand Canal, this time to stay, we come to the Palazzo Vendramini Calergi, where Richard Wagner died. We follow the Canal where, after crossing the Cannaregio, we discover the Church of San Geremia and the austere Palazzo Labia (16th century), which contains famous frescoes by Giovanni Battista Tiepolo.

Chiesa degli Scalzi

Church of the. Scalzi

Next to the railway station is the Church of the Scalzi with an 18th century facade. From here we take the ferry which will sail down the entire length of the Grand Canal and leave us at the Island of San Giorgio Maggiore, where there is a group of buildings dating from various periods, and dominated by the church designed by Andrea Palladio (1565-1980) which contains numerous paintings by Tintoretto and other artists.

We return to Piazza San Marco, where our Venetian tour comes to an end. It can be made more complete by taking four days for it, instead of two, following the same itineraries indicated above, but with detours and additions.

The Carnival

Carnival Masks

The Carnival is probably the biggest single event of the Venetian calendar. *Carnivale* runs for the ten days preceding Mardi Gras, and the entire city is given over to costumed revelry, impromptu street concerts, and pageants and balls of every kind. This is an experience you will treasure for a lifetime!

Where to have dinner in Venice

Restaurants in Venice:

* Dal Moro's - Fresh Pasta To Go Calle De La Casseleria, 5324 Castello, +39 327 870 5014: If you venture here you will see how good the pasta is. The people aren't wrong, there are quite a few sauces to select from & your total bill for 2x pastas can be only €10. The pasta is fresh, sauces were super tasty & the staff are very friendly. you can see why there was such a big line up to sample their goods. It's a very simple set up you order, get your pasta, eat it & go. No tables or chairs it's in and out.

* Ristorante Alle Corone Castello, Campo della Fava 5527 +39 041 241 0253: Alle Corone is in the Ai Reali Hotel, but it isn't like most hotel restaurants. This is first class all the way! The dining is rather formal but if that is what we desired for the occasion it's OK. You can have a very nice table at the window overlooking a canal and frequent gondolas.

* Torrefazione Marchi Rio Terra San Leonardo Cannaregio, 1337, +39 041 716 371: Coffee shop, highly recommend, super friendly staff and good variety. This smokes $3.50 for burnt coffee at Starbucks. this is great and not even 1 euro.

* Riviera Dorsoduro 1473 | Zattere - San Basilio, +39 041 522 7621: Small and a bit similar to most other places in town, with some 10-12 tables by the water, facing Giuddeca, Riviera is actually a true gem, where a simple meal becomes Michelin-star restaurant experience. Delicious starters with a special mention to a sashimi style special of eight fishes, all marinated in different ways.

* Bacareto Da Lele Campo dei Tolentini 183 - Santa Croce: Great little stand-up place with €1 small sandwiches and €0.60 glasses of wine. The owner is a character. Every so often he stops everything, pours a glass, toasts everybody and takes a drink. Lots of locals and tourists lined up and the guy in the back is madly making sandwiches and bringing them up as fast as he could. Nothing fancy, but they hit the spot.

* Osteria Alla Ciurma Calle Galeazza 406 - San Polo, +39 340 686 3561: Cicchetteria veneziana is the Venetian way of calling an aperitivo time with lovely 'tapas'. Nowhere else in Italy is that word being used. Linguistics aside, that place is a top notch aperitivo place. It's not a restaurant, it's a place you go for a quick Spritz aperol or Spritz Campari with the most amazing snacks/bites/ tapas/cicchetti you can find. Each one costs no more than €1,5 and are outside of this world. Try the 'gamberetti con lardo' (fried shrimps in lard), crostini con baccala (with cod fish), and fried fiori di zucca (fried courgette flowers). Try everything really. The shrimps in lard might sound like a heart attack on a stick, but it's so much worth it. Won't regret it I promise. Vegetarians switch beliefs after that!

* Prosciutto E Parmigiano Castello 5793, Calle Del Mondo Novo, +39 338.3120284: Like everything in Venice it is hard to find but well worth the search! The owner is very friendly offers samples of the meats and cheeses to

ensure you get what you like. He vacuum seals everything so it last longer if you want to take it away. It is a great snack for your train ride to Rome. Conveniently located between St. Mark's basilica and the Rialto bridge.

- Antico Forno Ruga Vecchia San Giovanni (Ruga Rialto) -970 | Between the Rialto Bridge and Campo San Polo, +39 041 520 4110: One of the best pizzas in Venice. Small, crowded, but worth it. This is pizza by the slice only, stand and eat only, so not for everyone, but if you love pizza....go. Two slices and beers under €15. Cheapest meal you can have in Italy. Try the margarita. The thin crust is tasty, cooked perfect, the sauce was excellent. Near the Rialto Bridge.

- Cafe Filermo Cannareggio 2208: Service, drinks and food here is excellent. When you walk in you are welcomed and served very well, the locals introduce themselves to you and give you tips and advice for the city. The man working here is an excellent ambassador for Venice.

- Osteria Al Squero Dorsoduro, 943/944, +39 335 600 7513: As the most of best places in Venice, this osteria is really small, with just a few seats inside. Most of the people are getting crostinis and drinks to sit outside on the canal. Their selection of cicchetti is great, and they are delicious! Priced at over a Euro each piece, they are well worth it. It's a great little gem for a refreshing beak in Dorsoduro. Try some with a glass of spritz or prosecco.

- La Colombina Corte del Pegoloto | Cannaregio 1828, +39 041 522 2616: This is a very authentic Venice experience of fine dining, you can taste things you've never had and find them delicious! The service is top-notch, it's recommended to anyone looking for a restaurant that is not a tourist trap. Order the tuna tartare for an appetizer and the baked creme tart w/ raspberries for dessert, both are some of the best food you can ever taste.

- Colpo de Mato Calle de la Laca 2465/f | Sestiere di San Polo, +39 041 524 2455: This is hard to find but it is worth it when you get there. Friendly staff and delicious food. Prices are reasonable. This is a small place. It's a bar/restaurant with seating inside and out. The pastas are great.

- Pasticceria Tonolo Dorsoduro, 3764, +39 041 523 7209: This place is great a for a quick standup breakfast. The coffee is so tasty and the wholemeal Croissants are scrumptious. You know when something is good when you find the locals in there too. For a quick, warm breakfast i would definitely recommend going here!

- Osteria - Enoteca Ai Artisti Fondamenta della Toletta Dorsoduro +39 041 523 8944: This restaurant has only 2 seatings in the evening - one at 7 PM and one at 9 PM. If you choose the 7 PM slot you must be finished by 9:00; if you choose the 9 PM slot you've got more time. The menu changes regularly and the food and wine are excellent. The wait staff is great and helpful. Overall a really nice place and really great food.

- All'Arco San Polo 436 | Calle Arco, +39 041 520 56 66: Fabulous, inventive cicchetti. This is the real thing - a tiny bar serving snacks at around 1 euro fifty. So many places offer a piece of bread with a shaving of Parma ham. At All' Arco there is a great variety of fish, cheese, various hams and sausage to top slices of crusty bread. The wines are equally good and so cheap! The service is delightful. No wonder the place gets packed!

• San Stae - Fontego delle Dolcezze Santa Croce 1910 - San Stae Street, +39 041 721424: This gelateria serves some of the best ice creams you can have. It is a very small shop in a corner, off the beaten path, near the Fashion Museum in Palazzo Mocenigo. This is a nice area of Venice, by the way. The ice cream is delicious and incredible value compared to other gelaterie

Lagoon Tour

Burano

Another Venice tourist attraction is a short distance from the historic city-cEnter and the itineraries frequented by mass tourism. In an area no less historic, no less genuinely Venetian, lie the islands of the lagoon in a wide expanse of water and marshlands where the quiet creeks change with the ebb and flow of the tide, and the traditional lagoon boats obstinately survive in the face of the aggressively noisy motor crafts.

The colors of the water, earth, and sky mix with the red brick of human constructions, and the sandbanks offer shelter to the typical fauna, dwarf herons,

herons, seagulls, hawks, and kingfishers... Here is a Venice where nature dominates, but where traces of history tell of the origins of the city itself and its distant past.

How to get there

There are many organized tours to the Lagoon Islands, I don't recommend taking one of them, you would be herded in a group rushing through the glass factories, and spending little time on the various islands. Going instead on your own, using public ACTV transportation you will save money, will have the time to spend in all the places that will appeal to you, and will have a much better experience.

To go, catch the ACTV boat line 12 or 13 at Fondamente Nove to Murano.

Murano

Murano Glass Sculpture

Glass has been made on the islands of the Venetian Lagoon for at least 1300 years. The industry had its beginnings in Torcello in the 7th or 8th century; production later shifted to Venice, where it remained concentrated until the *fornaci* or furnaces were moved to the island of Murano as a fire-prevention measure in 1291. Today, "Venetian glass" is a synonym for "Murano glass," and the island's glass industry is enjoying a resurgence under a new generation of master artists and craftsmen.

Murano Glass Factory

Public factory visits

The most interesting glass factories and ateliers on Murano aren't open to visitors, for two reasons:

- They're in the business of making glass, not entertaining tourists;

- Master glass artisans have spent years refining their proprietary techniques and don't want competitors taking notes.

Still, as you walk around Murano, you're likely to find mass-market *fornaci* or furnaces that welcome tourists. From the Colonna water-bus stop, turn left as you exit the boat platform and walk along the water until you reach a "Fornace

Glass" sign on a door below the Calle S. Cipriano street sign. Pass beneath the *"Fornace - Entrata Libera"* entrance sign, follow the sidewalk, and enter the factory to view a free glassmaking demonstration. (Afterwards, you'll exit through the showroom.) The demonstration takes less than 10 minutes, but it's interesting if you haven't seen a glass furnace.

Boat to Burano for lunch and browsing. One *vaporetto* line runs from Venice to Burano: the 12. The large express ferry runs from Venice's Fondamente Nove, to Murano and Burano. It takes about 45 minutes.

Burano

Burano

All visitors of Burano remain intrigued by the many colors of houses that are reflected in the green waters of channels, by the *Oblique Bell Tower*, by the tranquility and the calmness with which the elderly ladies embroider by their tombolo, while they are laughing and chatting in squares among them. It seems to be paradise. Children dart freely with their bicycles, there are balconies with multicolored flowers, fishermen who put up fresh fish from their traditional boats.

Burano is an island in the Northern Venetian Lagoon, 11 kms northeastern far from Murano and **Venice**, to which it is connected by the Canale Bisatto - Canale Carbonera - Scomenzera San Giacomo's trail: this route from Venice to Burano takes 45 minutes by boat.

One time ago fishing was the main job in Burano, while today it is tourism besides retail trade and restaurants. Burano is very famous for its lace, and there's a Lace Museum as well as shops selling lace. The women of the island have been experts at lace since the 1400s, when Leonardo da Vinci himself visited the shop for cloth that he used on the altar at the Duomo di Milano.

Entrance into the Lace Museum is included in the Museum Pass. Single tickets for just the Museum are sold onsite at 5.50 €, 4.00 € for seniors.

Shuttle boat to Torcello, tour the church, and then head back to Burano. From Burano it's a short boat ride on ACTV vaporetto line 9 to Torcello, a peaceful island whose cathedral has stunning Byzantine mosaics.

Where to eat in Burano

You'll eat better on Burano than almost anywhere in Venice

Restaurants in Burano:

- Al Gatto Nero Da Ruggero Fondamenta della Giudecca 88 +39 041-730-120: If you're thinking of seeing Burano on a trip to Venice, plan ahead and choose this restaurant. They've been established for many decades and know how to please.

- Devil Via San Mauro, 24, +39 041/735336: This little place on Burano looks like nothing special from the outside, but it can surprise you. The price is really good, one pizza is about 7-8€ and you wait about 5 minutes for yours. The pizza itself is delicious! Nice crust, very good topping. Seatings inside and outside is though limited.

- Al Fureghin Sestiere San Martino Sinistra, 888 +39 041 527 2250: Great lunch on Burano at an unpretentious little restaurant by the canal. Excellent value, (around twenty euro) for a fresh seafood platter that takes you to eat and very reasonably priced drinks.

- Ai Cesendeli Via San Martino sinistro 834 | Vicino Ponte Degli Assassini, +39 041730055: Decent pasta and pizza at a reasonable price. Service is friendly and efficient and the restaurant has a nice atmosphere, with the old local men popping in for a vino at the bar.

- Riva Rosa Ristorante Via San Mauro, 296, +39.041.730850: The food is delicious, the outdoor seating is in a picturesque setting and the indoor decor is very nice and contemporary. Service is excellent. Food fresh and delicious.

- Trattoria Raspo de Ua Via GalOppi 560, +39 041-73-00-95: From the outside, this place looks like nothing. Inside, there are three different themes, each room well appointed and remarkable. Altogether a great dining experience.

- Trattoria da Primo e Paolo Piazza Galuppi 285, +39.041.735550: There is plenty of competition for top-notch (and not cheap) food in Burano and Torcello (and even Mazzorbo, if you avoid the pretentious Venissa con-job), but what makes the difference is the place's management: A genuinely nice family formed by ex-Cipriani Paolo, his wife and three daughters, who spend their day off visiting area farmers for the best ingredients (hand-milled polenta from Eraclea!!) and their mornings choosing and preparing fresh seafood... These guys (gals mainly!) really care about their trade and their customers, who are warmly and sincerely welcomed. This is all a family restaurant should be (except for the prices, but this is Venice, and thus unavoidable).

• Pizzeria Spaghetteria Bar Sport San Martino Sinistro 286, +39.041.730003: Great place for lunch. Plenty of outdoor seating. Variety of food and drinks to choose from. The pizza is especially good. About a leisurely 15 mins walk into Burano from the Water bus stop, you will like that it is not on the main walk way, so it is peaceful while having your lunch.

• Ristorante Pizzeria Principe Fondamenta San Mauro, 455 +39 041 735067: Staff very friendly, helpful and fast. The place is excellent in the heart of Burano island. Food excellent and not expensive! Worth a visit!

• Pizzeria Trattoria Leon Coronato Piazza Galuppi, 314 +39 041 730230: Likely the only place the locals eat, excellent seafood and pizza. You will be presently surprised. Only downside is no credit card, but ATM/bank is next door so all good. Should really support places like these to make sure they stay around. Family owned.

• Fritto Misto Fermata Vaporetto: There might be seven kinds of seafood, battered and fried. This isn't haute cuisine; heck, it isn't even cuisine. It's just food. But it's fresh fish cleanly cooked, and it is delicious. And cheap.

• Ristorante Da Forner Fondamenta Terranova 130, +39 041 730002: A la carte, and set menus at 20 and 25 Euro. Morning/lunch only: Cash only; closed Wed Well worth seeking out, past the statue of Il Buranello, over the bridge - only one, but another under construction, and follow the canal as it curves round to the left. Much cheaper than Il Gatto Nero or Da Romano, which are of course excellent but pricey and get booked up.

• Al Vecio Pipa Strada San Mauro, 397, +39 041 730357: There are various fixed price menus available as well as a la carte. We had the menu del giorno at 25euro, which comprised an aperitivo and antipasto, primo, secondo, dessert plus wine and water (bottled).

• Laguna Bar Via San Martino 378, +39 393 239 9747: You can stop by Laguna Bar for a quick snack and enjoy toasted sandwiches and beer The sandwiches are delicious and very well filled, service prompt, friendly and attentive, and the prices very reasonable.It's not fine dining, but for what it is - thoroughly recommended.

• Pizzeria La Perla Via Galuppi 307, 39 041 735275: Pizza is prepared from scratch, and ready to eat in 5 minutes, simply delicious, and the owners very welcoming and helpful. A highly recommended option for lunch or light meal on Burano!

• Ai Pescatori Piazza B. Galuppi 371 +39 041 730650: Lovely find on Burano. Slightly away from the main street so a more authentic, quieter feel.

Attentive, knowledgeable and friendly waiters make the experience very pleasurable. We would advise to pre-book if you can to guarantee a table.

- Trattoria Caffe Vecchio Via S Martino dx 193: It has about twenty or so tables outside, and seating for a similar number inside behind sliding glass partitions should the weather take a turn for the worse.

- Bar Caffe Palmisano Via Galuppi: Nice quaint cafe on beautiful Burano. Nice selection of paninins, pizzas and mini rolls with generous meat fillings. Red wine was a steal at €2 a glass..... All in all a nice place for a little snack to rest those weary limbs but don't expect much personality from the staff!

- Quarta Generazione Ristorantino Via Galuppi 359: This small restaurant is on Galuppi street, the main one in Burano island of Venice. Most of the time this beautiful island is overcrowded, with hundreds of tourists filling the streets. The street is full of restaurants and embroidery shops. This restaurant offers very good light meals, including local dishes and pizzas. If you wish, you could order a full meal as well.

- Su e zo bar San Mauro 25, +39 342 356 8314: This little trattoria is handy to access and serves good food at reasonable prices (think €8.50 for a ham and mushroom pizza, €10 for spaghetti carbonara etc and not a huge amount more for larger meals such as sea bass). The owner/patron is a lively chap and you don't feel as though this is just another tourist trap.

- Restaurant Galuppi Via B. Galuppi 468-470: Eat at The Galuppi and seat outside enjoying the warm climate. The waiters are all very attentive and professional. The menu has a reasonable selection of Italian food and there are some items on the menu that are 'frozen' but' in fairness to the restaurant they are clearly marked telling you so.

Torcello

Church of Santa Fosca on Torcello Island.

Founded in the 5th century, Torcello is even older than Venice and was a very important island in ancient times, once having a population possibly around 20,000. Eventually malaria hit the island and much of the population either died or left. Buildings were plundered for building material so that little remains of its once splendid palaces, churches, and monasteries.

Torcello's cathedral was built in 639 and has a tall 11th century bell tower that dominates the skyline. Inside the cathedral are stunning Byzantine mosaics from the 11th to 13th centuries. One of the most impressive is the depiction of the *Last Judgement*.

Zip back to Fondamente Nove in 45 minutes.

Museum Pass

The Museum Pass is a combined entry to the Civic Museums currently open and those connected. (not including Palazzo Fortuny and the Clock Tower). It's valid for 6 months from the date of purchase and allows only one entry in each museum, also it can be picked up at any museum included in the pass and allows entry to the following museums:

Museums in Piazza San Marco

- Palazzo Ducale
- Museo Correr
- National Archaeological Museum
- Rooms of the Biblioteca Nazionale Marciana

Other Museums of Venice

- Ca 'Rezzonico Museum of Eighteenth Century Venice
- Carlo Goldoni's House
- Palazzo Mocenigo Museum and Study Center for the History of Textiles and Costumes
- Ca 'Pesaro International Gallery of Modern Art and Museum of Oriental Art
- Museum of Glass - Murano
- Lace Museum - Burano
- Museum of Natural History

Whole 24,50 € Reduced - senior discount (65 years+) 18,50 €. "Museum Pass" Family Offer: 1 admission fee and the others reduced for families of two adults and at least one child (aged 6 to 18 years). Under 6 years free.

Taking a gondola ride

Gondola

A 40-minute ride, which goes slowly, remember, so it's not like you'll see much of the city, starts at 80 € tip (after 7 pm, it's 100 € plus tip). Luckily that's not per person, but per boatful—the reason most gondolas are packed.

In summertime; Venice is very hot, very humid, and very smelly and being that close to the canal is not recommended.

A personal recommendation: hop a *traghetto* instead. These are gondola shells, meaning without all the seats and trappings, and for under a Euro you can stand in one to be transported with other locals across the Grand Canal, quickly and cheaply. Good balance is recommended though, since you'll be standing up in a little boat on a small waterway filled with water taxis. When walking through Venice, follow signs for "*Traghetti*" which will take you to a dead end at the canal, where the boat will pull up and you'll hand over a few coins.

Cicchetti bars

Wine *demijohn* ready for the cicchetti bar

Venice, once a European superpower, but today, is just a small town of about 60,000 people. Yet it has more than 10 million visitors a year. There are no restaurants left in Venice that don't rely on tourists. "*But there are still the cicchetti bars.*"

Venice has a wonderful tradition of *cicchetti* (pronounced chi-KET-tee) — the local appetizers that line the counters of little pubs all over town, but especially outside of the central tourist areas. You can visit a series of these characteristic hole-in-the-wall pubs, eating ugly-looking morsels on toothpicks, and washing it all down with little glasses of wine. An added advantage is that local characters surround you. And, in a town with canals and no cars, pub-crawling is safe and easy. Venetians call this pub crawl the *giro d'ombra*. Giro means stroll, and ombra — slang for a glass of wine — means shade.

Cicchetti bars have a social standup zone and a cozy gaggle of tables where you can generally sit down with your cicchetti or order from a simple menu. In some of the more popular places, the local crowds spill happily out into the street. Food usually costs the same price whether you stand or sit.

Chicchetti bars recommended

- I Chioschetto Dorsoduro 1406A
- Al Vapore Via Fratelli Bandiera 8
- Alla Palanca Giudecca 448
- Angiò Castello 2142
- Aurora San Marco 48-50
- Dogado Lounge Cannaregio 3660A
- Il Caffè Dorsoduro 2963
- La Mascareta Castello 5183
- Orange Dorsoduro 3054A
- Ai Do Draghi Dorsoduro 3665
- Ai Postali Santa Croce 821
- Al Pesador San Polo 125-6
- Al Prosecco Santa Croce 1503
- Ardidos Cannaregio 2282
- Area Club Via Don Tosatto 9
- Bacaro Jazz San Marco 5546
- Bar ai Nomboli San Polo 2717C
- Bar all'Angolo San Marco 3464
- Café Blue Dorsoduro 3778

Getting in

Because Venice is on a lagoon, the water plays a crucial role in transportation. The most popular way to approach Venice is by boat or train.

Getting in By plane

The closest airport is Marco Polo (ICAO: **LIPZ**), on the mainland near Mestre (a more typical Italian city, without Venice's unique structure).

There is another airport in Treviso, very small and 40 km (25 mi) from Venice.

Both airports have bus connections with Venice (Piazzale Roma), Mestre, Padua and other towns.

Marco Polo airport runs a shuttle bus to the Alilaguna water-bus jetty where €15 gets you a leisurely 1-hour boat trip to San Marco via Murano, Lido and the Arsenale.

Alternatively you can travel in style (and much faster) by hiring one of the speedy water-taxis for about €80.

Eurobus service/BASIQ-AIR Treviso Airport – Mestre-Venezia

Every day fast connection, by freeway, from/to S. Angelo Airport of Treviso with Mestre Railway and Venice (Piazzale Roma). The service is in connections with the departures and the arrivals of the BASIQ-AIR flights.

Eurobus service/RYANAIR Treviso Airport – Mestre-Venezia

Every day fast connection, by freeway, from/to S. Angelo Airport of Treviso with Mestre Railway and Venice (Piazzale Roma). The service is in connections with the departures and the arrivals of the RYANAIR flights.

Getting in By train

Trains from the mainland run through **Venezia Mestre** and to the **Venezia Santa Lucia** train station on the west side of Venice (make sure you don't get confused with Venezia Mestre which is the last stop on the mainland!).

Venezia Santa Lucia is Venice's Train Station. It is connected to the rest of Italy with Eurostar trains, Intercity and Interregional and local trains.

Inside the station there are trolleys for your luggage which can be taken up to the water-bus stop by using the side exit of the station, thus avoiding the steps outside the main exit.

You can leave your luggage at the left luggage office (near platform 14), open daily from 6am to midnight. If you need help transporting your luggage in Venice, you can phone the Cooperativa Trasbagagli (tel.+390415203070).

For detailed information on train timetables and ticket prices you can check the Public Railways website www.trenitalia.com, or the competing private company NTV, they run high-speed service from Rome and Florence to Venice.

From the Santa Lucia station, water buses (*vaporetti*) or water taxis can take you to hotels or other locations on the islands.

Getting in By car

Cars can arrive in Venice, but are left on the parking at the entrance to the city (Piazzale Roma or Tronchetto – Europe's largest car park.) Car parking is expensive here and the tailbacks can be quite large, an alternative is to use the car parks on the mainland (terra ferma) and catch a vaporetto or bus into Venice. A good idea is to park near the Mestre railway station and catch a train to Venezia S.Lucia; there are many trains, it is very near (8-10 minutes) and quite cheap. Besides, Venezia S.Lucia is a good starting point to visit Venezia.

It is easy to reach Venice by car with the following motorway and road connections: **A 4** from Trieste and from Turin, **A27** from Belluno, **A13** from Bologna, and the **state roads SS.309 Romea** from the Adriatic Coast, **SS.14** from Trieste, **SS.13** from Treviso, **SS.11 from Padua.** Venice is always clearly sign posted.

Once you have arrived near the lagoon, get on to the Ponte della Libertà – a long straight line with two lanes linking Venice to the mainland - follow the signs for Venice and you will arrive at Piazzale Roma. Here you have to leave your car and start your adventure in Venice, on foot or by water-bus.

Here are the **parking areas at Piazzle Roma**: the Autorimessa Comunale, the Garage S.Marco and the small open air car park S.Andrea.

One alternative is the **large car park on the Tronchetto Island**. From the Tronchetto Island you reach Venice by water-bus line 82.

Another possibility is **leaving your car in Mestre** – parking it in the small car parks before you reach the Ponte della Libertà or in those opposite to the railway station of Mestre and reach Venice by bus (Line 2) or by train (ten minutes ride). Once you have parked your car and therefore solved one of the main problems arriving in Venice, your adventure can start: on foot or by water-bus.

This is the list of Parkings in Piazzale Roma, Tronchetto and Mestre:

- ASM Venezia Piazzale Roma Garage (Loc. Piazzale Roma) tel. 0412727301
- Parking Sant'Andrea (Loc. Piazzale Roma) tel. 0412727304
- ASM Parking San Giuliano tel. 0415322632
- ASM Mestre Piazzale Candiani tel. 041976844-985616
- Venezia Tronchetto Parking (Isola del Tronchetto) tel. 0415207555
- Venezia Garage San Marco (Loc. Piazzale Roma) tel. 0415232213
- Fusina Park Terminal tel. 0415470160
- Tessera Park Marco Polo (Aeroporto di Marco Polo) tel. 0415415913
- Garage Europa (Mestre) tel. 041959202

Getting in By rental car

Most of the major rental car companies have outlets at Piazzale Roma, at the edge of the city. These are on the ground floor of one of the major parking stations. When you are dropping off your car, you need to find street parking and then walk to the hire car outlet and hand in the keys. Do not park in the parking station! There is a vaporetto stop across the road from the parking station.

Getting in By bus

The Piazzale Roma bus station is well served by vaporetti and water-taxis.

Getting in By boat

Ships arrive at the **Stazione Marittima** which is at the west end of the main islands, it is served by vaporetti and water taxis.

Getting around

Venice is a very walkable city, and the absence of cars makes it – mostly – a pleasant experience. The Rialtine islands – the 'main' part of Venice – are small enough to walk from one end to the other in about an hour.

If you want to get around a bit more quickly, there are numerous vaporetti (water buses) and water taxis.

Take a stroll on foot

You'll get to know all of its out of the way and unusual nooks and crannies, far off the more beaten paths. Distances are short: Get a map of the city, but don't bother to get "lost" in the back streets, bridges and campi (squares) that make up the real Venice.

Yellow signs, usually on the wall of a corner building, will direct you to the major spots. Keep right when walking in the city street. Never stop on bridges.

Do not be bewildered by "acqua alta" (flooding), you can still visit the city by using the wooden walkways.

Take the vaporetto (water bus ACTV public transportation)

You can buy the ACTV tickets at the ticket booths at the docks or the VE.LA. ticket offices. Tickets are not sold on board the boats. If you find yourself on board without a ticket, inform the ACTV crew immediately so as to avoid paying a fine.

You can also buy tickets from one of the many authorized sellers (tobacconists, newspaper stores and some cafés): remember to stamp your ticket in the yellow machine before getting on the vaporetto.

Venicecard is a ticket that allows you to use the main tourist services that the City offers to visitors.

At the boat stop there are maps depicting the directions all boats stopping there are going: the vaporetto is an easy way to admire all the mansions and buildings that overlook the Grand Canal and the lagoon.

The vaporetti are generally the best way to get around, even if the service route map changes frequently. If you are going to be in Venice for a few days visiting, it is a lot cheaper to get the vaporetti than to get private water taxis. If you want to have a romantic ride along the canals take a gondola ride.

ACTV runs the vaporetti and other public transport services both in the lagoon and on the terra firma. 1 day, 3 day and 7 day Venice Cards are available, in two variations (Blue and Orange). The basic Blue cards provide unlimited travel on the ACTV travel services (vaporetti, motoscafi and buses) and free use of the AMAV staffed toilets. The Orange card also provides free entrance to some of the museums (those covered by the Museum Card). Note that neither card includes the Alilaguna water-bus which serves Marco Polo airport unless you pay a surcharge.

Cross the Grand Canal on (Traghetti) ferry crossing

You can feel the excitement of a gondola ride cheaply by using the ferry crossings that link the various parts of the two sides of the Grand Canal. Venetians use this transportation when they need to move quickly from one side of the Grand Canal to another without crossing one of its three bridges. There is a gondola ferry at San Marcuola, Santa Sofia, San Tomà, San Samuele, Santa Maria del Giglio, and the Dogana.

Where to buy souvenirs in Venice.

Souvenir Mask hop in Venice

Venice is a minefield when it comes to buying souvenirs and it pays to be wary.

There is the glass shop in Calle della Cortesia which sells genuine Murano glass with certificate and provenance of the goods.

For leather there is the shop on Rialto on the San Polo side.

Also the glass shop in Campo San Fantin with the leather shop next door. Here you can buy some unusual souvenirs, the most delicate bookmarks, bottle openers and beautiful notebooks with hand made paper.

For jewelry with Venetian motifs then the shop in Campo San Luca, not cheap but then again not overly expensive.

It is possible to buy paintings and sketches from some of the artists and once again these are not overly priced but watch before you buy, as there is a fair amount of fakery. Go with your instinct.

If you would like a mask then go to a place where you can see them being made rather than by something made who knows where. If you find yourself in Campo San Barnaba, then leave by the metal bridge by the church. Go straight along, turn right and left and you will see a mask workshop.

If you would like Burano lace then this is more difficult. The romantic image of fishermen's' wives on Burano happily lace making and singing to their menfolk out at sea is nice, but in the present days not really realistic if you wish to buy said lace. However you can buy genuine Burano lace, (the operative word when buying Venetian souvenirs is 'genuine') but you will have to search for it and not rely on a sign in a window saying that it is so.

However, for some fun gifts or mementos that all ages can play with, try the shop in Campo San Barnaba on the corner by the floating grocery barge. They have lots of witty wooden sculptures and mobiles with a Venice theme.

You could buy direct from a local craftsman such as the Bottega di Costantini (Calle del Fumo, 5311 in the Cannaregio district). It is located in a narrow lane between Campiello Widman and the Fondamente Nuovo vaporetto stop. The incredible window display of glass insects, birds, and sea life caught our attention.

The owner/artist, Vittorio Costantini, was born on Burano and his glass insects have been featured in museums and galleries all over the world. If you stop by the shop, you can watch him create his amazing specimens using glass rods and a special torch, and also admire his own personal glass menagerie. I swear, if you saw one of his glass bugs on your floor at home, you would stomp on it without a second thought. They look that real.

Consider also:

- Scarves: light, easy to pack, and available in tons of colors and fabrics.

- Ceramics: hand-painted kitchenware is an Italian tradition. Larger items can usually can be shipped.

- Books: nice picture guidebooks from the gift shops of museums you visit - especially those which do not allow photos - are great keepsakes when you get home

- Music: CD's offered by street musicians you may have enjoyed

- Art: a small drawing or watercolor piece from a street artist

- Italian soccer or bike jerseys: also lightweight and packable, fans of the sports will love them

- T-shirts: not a thing wrong with one if you'll wear it later. Choose well-made products with images of your favorite attractions

- Biscotti or amaretti cookies, licorice or other wrapped, Italian sweets. Also dried pasta.

- We always pick up a Christmas ornament when we travel to a new destination. Putting up the 'Travel Tree' is an event at our house that brings back lots of great memories.

One day trip to Verona

The Arena

With its position between the banks of the River Adige winding at the foot of the hills, the beauty of its colors, the green of its cypresses, the dark red of its bricks, the ivory of its stone, the white marbles, the extraordinary barroom; of its mixture of Roman, medieval and Renaissance art, and the magnificent splendor of its churches, Verona is one of the most fascinating cities of Italy. An ancient prehistoric settlement, then a city of the Gauls and the Romans, a capital of Ostrogoth, Longobard, and Frankish dynasties, it next passed, after the age of the communes, into the brief, but happy, possession of the Scaligers (1260-1387) and lastly to the Venetian Republic.

Our visit begins in the spectacular Piazza Bra, the site of the enormous Roman Arena (1st century), the largest structure of its kind after the Colosseum.

Next to the Arena, we find the neoclassical Palazzo Municipale. (Town Hall) and, set against the city walls, the Palazzo della Gran Guardia (1610).

The palace served as the headquarters and registered office of the city guard and was built in 1610.

The loggia and the parade ground on the ground floor of the palace were designed by Domenico Curtoni. The staircase and upper floor were not completed until 1850. You can see the style of the master builder of Curtoni, Sanmicheli, especially when looking at the twin pillars on the upper floor – they imitate Sanmicheli's Porta Palio.

Today, the former city guard is used as a conference cEnter and as a gallery.

Palazzo della Gran Guardia

Passing through the 15th century archways which span Corso Ports Nooks, we come upon the Museum of Gems and Jewelry, with a handsome classical courtyard; beyond Via Roma is a row of three fine palaces, Vaccari, Barbaro and Malfatti (designed by Sanmicheli, 1555).

Taking Via Roma, we reach Castelvecchio, an impressive 14th century fortress on the Adige, which today houses the Civic Museum and its important collection of Venetian painting (works by G. Bellini, Crivelti, Tintoretto, Titian, Tiepolo, Guardi, and by those gentlest of Veronese artists, Stefano da Zesio and Altichicro).

Before leaving the Castle, we should wander among its towers and battlements to enjoy the marvelous view.

Taking Stradone Antonio Procolo, we pass by the Renaissance church of San Bernardino (1466), and come to San Zero, the most beautiful church in Verona and one of the most important in Italy. It was founded in the 5th century, but in its present form it dates from 1138, at which time the magnificent face was finished with its elegant porch and carvings by Nicola and Guglielmo, a masterpiece of Romanesque sculpture.

San Bernardino

Passing through the superb Romanesque bronze doors, we enter the grandiose interior where, on the high altar, there is a Triptych by Andrea Mantegna (1459), one of the noblest paintings of the Renaissance.

Following the Adige back to Castelvecchio, we go on by it to the superb Arco dei Gavi (ca. 50 AD.), demolished in 1805 by the French and later rebuilt. After the Palazzo Canossa, designed by Sanmicheli, we go on down Corso favor where we find, on the left, the Romanesque church of S. Lorenzo, and on the right, the Palazzo Bevilacqua (1530) and the church of SS. Apostoli.

Beyond the Roman Ports Borsari, we come to the Torre del Gardello, in front of which we find the lively Piazza delle Erbe, whence we pass into the adjoining Piazza dei Signori, a superb creation dating from the Middle Ages (Palazzo della Ragione, 1193, and the 13th century Palazzo degli Scaligeri) and from the Renaissance (the splendid Loggia).

Torre del Gardello

Close by here is one of the most enchanting spots in Verona, that stretch of street dominated by the Arche Scaligere, in which, between their palace and S. Maria Antics are buried the Scaligeri lords, under whose rule Verona passed out of the Middle Ages into its glorious a Rebirth.

Wandering through the neighboring streets, we come to Juliet's House; then taking Via Stella, we pass be side the 14th century church of S. Maria delta Scala, and then along Via Anfiteatro, with the Palazzo dei Diamanti, we return to Piazza Bra, where we may interrupt our tour for lunch in one of the excellent restaurants.

San Fermo Maggiore

In the afternoon, we start off again from Piazza Bra and going to the left of the Town Hall, reach the very ancient church of San Pietro Incarnario and then San Fermo Maggiore (1261), richly decorated inside with frescoes by Altichievo and with magnificent tombs. From San Fermo, we cross the Adige on the Prime Navi, beyond which is the handsome Palazzo Pompeii (1530) designed by Sanmicheli, and then the Church of San Paolo (inside, canvases by Veronese, Caroto, etc.).

North of Via Venti Settembre is the church of SS Nazaro and Celso (fine Venetian paintings), from which we make our way to S. Maria in Organo, an 8th century Benedictine abbey remodeled by Sanmicheli (superb inlaid woodwork in the choir dating from 1499).

Passing Santa Chiara (15th century) on our right, we reach the foot of St. Peter's Hill, into the side of which is set the Roman Theatre, in a magnificent position overlooking the city and the curving sweep of the Adige. Nest to it is the Archaeological Museum.

San Giorgio

Following the curve of the Adige, we come to the stately church of San Giorgio (1477-1536) which contains several famous paintings, amongst them the Martyrdom of St. George, a masterpiece by Veronese, and the Baptism of Christ by Tintoretto.

Crossing the bridge in front of the Roman Theatre, only a few steps away we find the Romanesque Cathedral with its lovely semicircular apse (12th century) and a Cloister with small red marble columns; inside, the Assumption by Titian (1540). We then take Via Damon and come to the last masterpiece of Veronese architecture which remains to be seen, Sant'Anastasia, a Dominican Gothic church (1290) with priceless frescoes by Pisanello.

Verona has a ancient historic center, very extensive and well conserved. Roman municipality of the 49 B.C., reserves important tracks of that prosperous period. The roman amphitheater called the Arena, one of the most famous outdoor theatre in the world, the Roman Theatre, the Gavi Arch and the monumental gates (Porta Borsari and the Porta dei Leoni) are grand works designed to last millennia.

Noteworthy architectural works remain from the Scaligeri Seigniory and from the Austrian domination during the Risorgimento, but there are also, palaces and squares of every epoch and style in warm soft colors.

Verona Arena

The churches of the town are numberless and of great historical and artistic value. Some of the most important are: the Basilica of San Zeno, a perfect example of Romanesque architecture, is dedicated at the Saint Patron of the town and the panels of bronze that adorned the wooden doors, are a work of the local sculpture.

The churches of San Fermo, Santi Apostoli and San Lorenzo date back to the same period while the church of Sant'Anastasia was built during the the Scaligers' Seignory and is the home of fresco masterpieces by Pisanello and Altichiero. The church of San Giorgio is attributed to Sanmicheli, an architect who worked at several of the most important palaces and fortresses of the city.

A small marble balcony records the most famous verses of Shakespeare tragedy, in which Romeo declares his love for Juliet, Shakespeare's immortal heroine, as she stands on it. The building, which probably dates back to the XIII century, has a brick facade and large tribolate windows; following the tradition it is the house where the beautiful Juliet lived. Her tomb is located instead in an old monastery and the place is imbued with an intensely romantic atmosphere.

Juliet Balcony

The other eternal symbol of Verona is the Arena: the magnificence of the roman ruins, the perfection of the staging and the musical shows give to the performances of the Arena that inimitable tone which since 1913 has been attracting big crowds of spectators to one of the most prestigious opera seasons.

Every year the rich program includes works, concerts and ballets. Verona offers also many folklore events between which the "Bacanal del Gnoco", the Veronese carnival, arrived at the 475^ edition.

Around Verona

Verona

The territory of the Scaligeri province is embraced from north-west at south-east by the Adige river: about ten of bridges connects the two parts of the town, but in the roman period Verona had only two bridges: the Pons Postumius (doing not more exist), and the Pons Marmoreus. This last, known like Ponte Pietra, destroyed during the Second World War, was rebuilt using the original parts; suggestive also the Ponte Scaligero, in the neighborhood of Castelvecchio, also it, like the previous, exclusively to pedestrian use, was built and fortified during the Seignory of Della Scala for civic and military purposes.

The territory around of Verona is rich of history: there is not in fact one Veronese town which cannot boast at least one stately residence or a medieval castle or the memory of some important past events. Soave, Villafranca, Cologna Venetam Valeggio sul Mincio, are some of the most significant examples of this heritage,

Around at those and other centers are extended the fertile Veronese plain, in the South part called also "Basso Veronese", rich of products of the agriculture, of handcrafting tradition and important firms. Its delicate and poetic landscape should not be overlooked, especially during autumn.

Mount Baldo

The chain of the Mount Baldo arises at north-west in comparison with the town and, in the last centuries was called, from botanists and naturalists "Hortus Europae" for the extraordinary variety of flora species, more of which endemic.

Appeared on the lake of Garda like a incomparably beautiful balcony, the mountain can be easily reached also with the new cableway that covers the route between Malcesine and the Mount Baldo with a inequality of 1650 meters, in only 10 minutes.

The north-east zone of the territory is occupied from the Natural Park of the Lessinia, built of recent, in the 1990, that exploits the naturalistic-surrounding importance of this plateau which has witnessed in the XIII century the settlement of Bavarian-Tirolose speaking Cimbric communities and has developed important summer and winter tourism. Some of its most interesting attractions are the Fossil Remains Museum in Bolca which is dedicated to precious fossil fish of tropical climate, found in the "Pesciara", a fossil deposit of the Tertiary Era and considered, in its kind, between the most important in the world; the Ponte of Veja, a big rocky arch recognized like natural monument; the Molina Falls park which contains marvelous waterfalls and tiny green lakes, nature trails. Moreover the plateau offers, possibility of strolls, excursions, mountain bike, trekking, free-flying, horse-riding and during the winter season it becomes a big ski area.

The north-west boundaries of the provincial territory is delimited from the shores of the lake of Garda: that its light and colors combines the fascination of the Mediterranean landscape with the atmosphere of nordic fiords. The east shore, known like Riviera degli Ulivi, offers culture, story and traditions, like testify, the Romanesque churches, Scaligeri castles, residences in the Venetian style and nineteenth-century fortifications which stand on its sides or in the surroundings; it is the ideal place for the sojourn of people fond of sport and active holidays, perfect to practice, sailing, canoeing, wind-surf, fishing and immersions, but also so much cheerfulness with the fun-fairs, natural parks and fields from golf.

Where to eat in Verona

- <u>La Bottega della Gina</u> Via Fama 4/c, +39 045 594725 Great "fast food" place with handmade art like pasta! Besides tortellini it also serves other pasta and different lunch dishes. Small , not very fussy place, but not only the food is great, but you can also see it done before your eyes.

- <u>Borsari 36</u> Corso Porta Borsari, 36, +39 045 590566 The restaurant is hidden in a small courtyard at Corso Porta Borsari 36. The service and knowledge of the Maitre D is good. The caring service includes the allergies code in case you want to know and they will cook accordingly to you need. The wine list is so extensive and is thick like a bible. The presentation of food is nice and serve with a complimentary starter, sorbet and petit four at the end. Price is reasonable.

- <u>Ghiotto Take Away</u> Via C. Abba 13/g +39 340 079 2112 The couple that runs the place are one of the most warm-hearted, good-humored people you'd ever meet in Verona, you step into their tiny domain to grab a bite and end up finding out the story of their lives, the next thing you know, you're sharing a laugh and indulging yourself with pizza. Believe it or not, the food is just as good, one would never guess that vegan food can be so exciting in its simplicity, super delicious and even kind of inventive. You should definitely come for good food and great company. They've been opened just about few months or so and (no surprise there) have already become a hit. They bake with inspiration and gib heart, trust me, it shows.

- <u>La Griglia</u> Via Leoncino, 29, +39 045 8031212 This restaurant is a trattoria so the interiors have typical Italian rustic charm and the food is simpler in presentation but everything is good and service friendly and warm. The location is actually just behind the Verona roman amphitheater, Arena di Verona, on the other side away from Piazza Bra. It's just a few steps away from where they place the Aida sets before the Opera season. It looks further than it really is on google maps and you can walk a shorter way if you know where it is. The easier way is to head to the entrance of the Arena, walk around along its perimeter in an anticlockwise direction and look out for Via Leoncino, somewhere on the right.

- <u>Osteria Barucchi</u> via Giacomo Barucchi 88, +39 339 624 6509 Well-managed and well-stocked Osteria, with the chance to taste in peace and quiet tranquility wine and a variety of craft beers and cold cuts and cheeses with fine details. Music in the evening and several events are organized around the time of the year by the owner very nice and well prepared. Recommend also for aperitif and after dinner.

- <u>Antica Torretta</u> Piazza Broilo 1, +39 045 80.15.292 Fantastic flavors and ingredients produce a great experience in an elegant indoor setting. Nestled in a quiet part of Verona with some of the most attentive waitstaff present is a great place to bring someone you love. The chef makes the effort to entice you with his creativity. The portions are small but of the highest quality. Each bite is savored as an individual experience. The wine list is excellent as well.

- Nastro Azzurro Vicolo Listone 4, +39 045 8004457 Pizza served outside in an atmospheric setting just off the Piazza Bra. Really tasty pizza, attentive, efficient staff. Though not in the piazza, but in a side street on the edge of it, the location is a delight, particularly if you reserve a table with a view of the Arena. The food is good and the menu varied. However what makes the difference is the service. The staff are friendly, knowledgeable and efficient. they seem to be just as happy to serve a quick pizza or a more fancy meal.

- Enoteca Segreta Vicolo Samaritana, +39 045 801 5824 out of the way but not too far off the main piazza Erbe, this place has a nice outside courtyard as well as an atmospheric cellar like inside. Food is beautiful, service friendly and very reasonable. Don't miss the dessert. It's nicely tucked away at the end of a tiny, out of the way street, so there's lots of atmosphere before you even enter. There's a sweet alfresco area on a deck out the front and a cellar downstairs. The place is off the beaten track and apparently very popular with the locals. The food is tasty, wines - great and the atmosphere friendly and perfect for a romantic dinner.

- Trattoria Dal Gal Via Segala Don Gregorio, 39/A, +39 045 890 0966 Leonardo the owner runs an amazing restaurant and has lovingly refurbished it offering the highest quality Italian food and wine with impeccable service. The restaurant is hidden away in a residential area so do not be alarmed that you have taken the wrong road.

- Vecio Macello Via Macello 8, +39 045 803 0348 The fish tasting menu is fabulous. 15 different fish and shellfish to try including an oyster. The tuna is excellent and the scallop adorable. Then just to finish it off you can have a plate of pasta with the ravioli to die for. The house wine for 12 euros is also excellent. The waiting staff is attentive and uses smiles rather than English to make you welcome .

How to get to Verona

The best way to get to Verona from Venice is by **train**. Direct service departs every half hour and take anywhere from 1 hour and 10 minutes to 2 hours and 20 minutes, depending on the type of train you catch. Tickets cost range from 8,60 € to 23 € one-way. From the Verona Porta Nuova station there is a 15 minutes walk to the center. There is a taxi stand just in front of the station, and there are also frequent local buses connections to the center. You find the schedule of the trains and buy tickets on the web site www.trenitalia.com. Enter **Venezia Santa Lucia** for the station in Venice and **Verona Porta Nuova** for Verona.

To arrive or to depart directly from Verona: The Verona Villafranca **airport,** located very near the center of the city, is connected to many European cities, specially during summertime. The City Center and Verona Porta Nuova Railway Station are connected with the **Aerobus**: From the Verona Airport to Verona Porta Nuova train station the shuttle service operates daily, at 5.35 am, 6.30 am, then every 20 minutes until 8.30 pm, and every 40 minutes until 11.10 pm. The shuttle service from Verona Porta Nuova train station to Verona airport operates daily, at 5.15 am, 6.10 am, then every 20 minutes until 8.10 pm, and every 40 minutes until 10.50 pm. The journey takes 15 minutes. www.aeroportoverona.it/en/

Arriving to Verona by **car**: the autostrada A4 passes through Verona coming from Milan in the west and going to Venice-Mestre in the east. The autostrada A22 passes through Verona coming from the Brenner Pass - Bolzano from the North and going to Bologna - Rome to the South.

One day trip to Vicenza

Villa Capra "La Rotonda"

Vicenza, which after evolving historically in much the same way as Verona, blossomed anew under Venice (from 1404). While Verona has a largely medieval aspect, Vicenza appears as a distinctly Renaissance town, mostly due to the efforts of its most important son, Andrea Palladio.

We enter the city, pass the Salvi Gardens (be beyond the gardens, the Loggia Valmarana and the Loggia dei Longhena), through the turreted Ports Castello and find ourselves in Corso Palladio, a fine street cutting Vicenza from one end to the other.

To the left is the Palazzo Bonin (formerly Thiene), designed by Scamozzi; across the way, Palazzo Bizzarri-Malvezzi. Turning left into Corso Fogazzaro, we come to the Franciscan Romanesque-Gothic church of S. Lorenzo, with an interesting doorway and a well-lit interior, its various chapels adorned with ancient frescoes and tombs of San Biagio illustrious citizens.

Following Contra Pedemuro-San Biagio we arrive in Contra Porti, with its magnificent palaces: to the right the Gothic Casa Porto-Scaroni and Palazzo Biego now Porto Festa (1552) designed by Palladio (Inside, frescoes by Tiepolo), and the Venetian-Gothic Palazzo Colleoni-Porto; to the left, Casa Trissino, now Sperotti, restored after air-raid damage in World War II the most beautiful Gothic palace in the town, and the Renaissance palace, Casa Porto, rebuilt after air-raid damage.

Then to the right again, comes Palazzo Thiene, with its terracotta doorway. After this introduction to the architecture of Vicenza, we come into the extraordinary Piazza dei Signori with the famous Basilica, designed by Palladio (1549), the charming Loggia dei Capitanio, also by Palladio, and the long Lombard palace of the Monte di Pieta', which incorporates the Baroque facade of S. Vincenzo.

Two columns support, in the Venetian manner, one a statue of the Saint and the other the Lion of St. Mark, emblem of the Venetian Republic. Passing along one side of the Basilica, we come to Piazza delle Erbe. with its medieval Tower, and then, to Piazza delle Biade, with the Gothic church of S. Maria dei Servi.

We come back and turn right up Corso Palladio (to the left, on the corner is the Gothic Palazzo da Schio) and into Contra Santa Corona, with the Romanesque church of Santa Corona, of brick with an imposing marble doorway. Inside, we see a Baptism of Christ by Giovanni Bellini, an Adoration of the Magi by Veronese and the magnificent Valmarana Chapel by Palladio.

After a short walk we come to two of Palladio's most inspired creations, in the square at the far end of the Corso- The first of these is the Teatro Olimpico, which he began shortly before his death and which was complete roofed by Scamozzi (1583), and which is the first theatre of modern times; and the second is the Palazzo Chiericati (1550), containing the two principal collections of the city: the important Archaeological Collection (with a magnificent Bacchus, of the school of Praxiteles) and the Art Gallery, which contains, besides a fine collection of works by local painters (Montagna, Buonconsigli, Mattei, etc.), some important canvases by Cima da Conegliano, Lotto, Veronese, Bassano, Tintoretto, Van Dyck, the wonderful Diana by Pittoni, pictures by Tiepolo (the immaculate) and Piazzetta, and a Flemish masterpiece: Calvary by Hans Memling.

By way of Via J. Cabianea, we reach Palazzo Godi, designed by Scamozzi (1569), and, from here, the Casa Pigafetta, a magnificent example of florid Gothic architecture, where the famous navigator was born. We then continue down to the Piazza del Duomo, to the Gothic Cathedral with a dome by Palladio (inside, a Polyptych by L. Veneziano) and to the courtyard of the Bishop's Palace, with its elegant Renaissance Loggia.

Leaving the city, we now climb the hill upon which stands the Basilica di Monte Berice, in order to admire, in the Refectory, a masterpiece by Veronese: The Banquet of Gregory the Great (1572). Leaving Monte Barico, and turning right, after some 500 yards., we come to the 17th century Villa Valmarana where Tiepolo painted (1757) what is one of the most important series of frescoes of the 18th century. Nearby is the Rotondo, Palladio's most beautiful villa, which has been the model for hundreds of neoclassical buildings in France, England and America.

Palazzo Thiene

Where to eat in Vicenza

Restaurants in Vicenza:

- Ristorante Il Querini da Zemin Viale del sole, 142, +39 0444 552054 To savor the flavors of the traditional local Vicenza food and enjoy delicious combinations on the advice of the professional staff and friendly.

- Il Ceppo Corso Palladio, 196 | Centro Storico Vicenza, +39 0444 544414 This restaurant specializes in baccala. Well cooked and not salty. Pleasant environment, friendly owner who gives you a potted history of the restaurant's links to the baccala' processing business. Slightly cramped but definitely worth a visit and definitely worth the price.

- Trattoria Zamboni via S.Croce, 73 Lapio di Arcugnano, +39 0444.273079 The restaurant is perfect. The atmosphere great. The air very clean. The service personals very kind. Foods extremely delicious.

- Il Molo Contra Pedemuro San Biagio, 48, +39 328 8087598 They don't have a typical menu that you read - the waiters will talk you through the different choices for the courses. Plus you get complimentary water and prosecco!

The villas in the province of Vicenza

Villa Capra "La Rotonda"

Along the roads around Vicenza, half-hidden, behind rich vegetation, often not seen by the hurried traveler, the are many buildings reminding the past times when living and spending hours at home and in the country meant intense pleasure: The villas in the province of Vicenza.

Some of them of incomparable splendor, others of modest make, some perfectly restructured in their original beauty, others neglected and weather-beaten, constitute the original diversity of the Province of Vicenza.

Andrea Palladio has left the prestigious sign of an unrepeatable time, when the munificence of a few great families has matched with the technical skills of humble artisans whose work, together with the genius of the great architect, has left one of the best examples of human inventiveness.

Palladio is an uni-cum, but many architects have followed his path by accepting or defying his inheritance: Scamozzi, Muttoni, Pizzocaro and other less famous which makes of our province a constant goal for visitors

How to get to Vicenza

The best way to get to Vicenza from Venice is by **train**. Direct service departs every half hour and take anywhere from 40 minutes to 1 hours and 20 minutes, depending on the type of train you catch. Tickets cost range from 6,00 € to 19 € one-way. From the Vicenza station there is a 5-10 minutes walk to the center. You find the schedule of the trains and buy tickets on the web site www.trenitalia.com. Enter **Venezia Santa Lucia** for the station in Venice and **Vicenza** for Vicenza.

By car: take the A4 autostrada highway that connects Venice with Milan, Vicenza is at 75 km from Venice. There are several large car parks that skirt the historic center, including the underground Park Verdi, just north of the train station, that you should enter from Viale dell'Ippodromo.

One day trip to Padua

A great one day trip from Verona is the city of Padua, with the Brenta Riviera villas. While Padua can be reached easily with the train from Verona, a car is recommended for this visit, as the villas are outside of downtown Padua.

In Padua take the National Highway no. 11, which runs along the banks of the Brenta. Here the great Venetian families built their famous country villas which, taken as a body, constitute the most important example of residential architecture in existence.

Villa Pisani maze

We can neither describe nor list them. They follow one another in uninterrupted succession, all more or less celebrated, up to the outskirts of Padua. Most worthy of being seen is the Villa Foscari (known as the Malcontenta), in a romantic and secluded position on the road to Fusina.

The astonishing series of villas, built over a span of 300 years, goes on, through the towns of Cringe, Mira, and Dean: at Stra is the celebrated Villa Pisani (1756), now belonging to the State, with its magnificent park, its maze, and its sumptuous interior, where many crowned heads have stayed, including Napoleon.

Particularly noteworthy is the glowing fresco painted by Tiepolo at the age of 66 on the ceiling of the reception-hall.

Sant'Antonio

PADUA, another city which, after its Roman origins and a turbulent medieval existence, achieved a happy equanimity under Venetian rule. We enter the city by way of Piazzale Stanga, going immediately (by Via Ognissanti and Via Belzoni) to S. Sofia, the oldest church in Padua (1125) with a magnificent apse.

From here we go to the Scrovegni Chapel, a small Gothic church in the garden which now occupies the site of the Arena, the ancient Roman amphitheater. It contains the cycle of 38 frescoes, which constitute a gigantic undertaking by Giotto (1305-6): it is from here, one might say, that Italian painting set out on its long journey down the ensuing centuries.

Crossing the garden, we come to the Church of the Eremitani (1276), once another sanctuary of Italian painting, before Allied bombs (1944) almost completely destroyed the frescoes by Andrea Mantegna which decorated it; important fragments of them still exist, however.

From here, we go towards the center of the town, passing by the Caffe Pedrocchi, a picturesque neoclassical building, and one of the few old Italian cafes still in existence, to three charming squares, one after the other: Piazza dei Frutti, delle Erbe, and dei Signori. Between the first two, rises the harmoniously elegant Palazzo della Ragione, an oblong building with an arcade, a loggia and a curved roof (1218-1306).

In Piazza dei Signori, we see the elegant Loggia della Gian Guardia (1523) and the Palazzo (del Capimnio, with its Clack Tower, whose arcade leads into the Corle Capitaniato and into the nearby square of the same name. Once the Carraresi Castle, belonging to the lords of Padua, Stood on the site of the Liviano, with rooms originally painted by Altichiero and Guariento.

Nearby is the handsome Vabaresso Arch, built in 1632 in honor of a Venetian mayor. We then enter the Piazza del Duomo, containing the Cathedral, with its rough unfinished facade and its plan based originally on designs by Michelangelo. To the right of the Cathedral is a beautiful Romanesque Baptistery (1260) containing a magnificent Poly-pitch and Frescoes by Giusto de' Menabuoi (1378).

In the nearby Via Vescovado, we come upon one of the most beautiful private residence in Padua, the House of Mirrors, so-called because of its polished polychrome marble surface. Returning to our previous route, we pass by the Town Hall and reach the ancient Palazzo dell'Universitá with its attractive 16th century courtyard.

Going down Via Roma and turning into the quaint Riviera dei Pomi Romani, we come to the square before the Basilica di Sant'Antonio. This church which presents a fascinating mixture of styles with its Gothic Romanesque walls and the oriental aspect of its seven domes, contains an immense collection of art tress ores, including the marvelous High Altar by Donatello. Also by Donatello is the elegant equestrian statue al' the Italian soldier of fortune, Erasmo da Norm, known as Gattamelata, which stands in front of the Basilica.

Prato della Valle Square

After visiting the church, the lovely cloister and the Museum of St. Anthony, we proceed to the adjacent Civic museum, which has a fine archaeological section, but most of all an excellent collection of paintings (works by Giotto, Lorenzo Veneziano, Jacopo and Giovanni Bellini, Foppa, Vivarini, Morone, Giorgione, Titian, Tintoretto, Veronese, Van Dyck, Piazzetta, Tiepolo, Ricci, Longhi, etc.).

Crossing the canal and going through the picturesque Botanical Gardens, we come into the elegant Prato della Valle, ornamented with canals, statues, trees and obelisks, an ingenious and poetical creation of the 18th century. From here, we move on to the imposing Church of S. Giustina, one of the largest in Christendom (16th century), containing numerous works of art. The Martyrdom of St. Justina by Veronese is in the apse.

Where to eat in Padua

Restaurants in Padua:

- Ristorante Belle Parti Via Belle Parti 11, +39 0498 751822 Fantastic food in a fantastic place washed down with wonderful wine from the vin yards at Montecchia, grown by Count Giordano Emo Capodilista. Well worth a visit when you are in Padua. Helpful and attentive staff made this a restaurant to remember.

- La Folperia Piazza della Frutta 1, +39 347 570 1232 Not a food truck as we know in US, but a food stand in easy to find location. Great to see what there daily specials are and add a couple of other items - sit down order a drink for bar next to stand and enjoy yourself and people watching.

- Enotavola Via dell'Arco 37, +39 0498 762385 The welcome is nice, the vibe is young, the wine selection is deep and there are really u unusual options, like a combination of tuna, duck and cabbage, perfectly balanced. Portions are on the small side but quality is high.

- Vecchio Falconiere Via Umberto I, 31/1, +39 049 656544 You can't even tell that it is a restaurant from the outside, but well worth entering. Friendly staff and fabulous local food and wine. Try their mixed meat specialty which is cooked at your table.

- Idea Pizza via Ognissanti 14, +39 0498 075240 It's a very small space (one table only), but the pizza is very good! Different choices of pizza, vegetarian also Staff very friendly and speaks English.

How to get to Padua

The best way to get to Padua from Venice is by **train**. Direct service is available with one to nine trains per hour and take anywhere from 25 minutes to 50 minutes, depending on the type of train you catch. Tickets cost range from 4,10 € to 17 € one-way. From the Padua station there is a 5-10 minutes walk to the center. You find the schedule of the trains and buy tickets on the web site www.trenitalia.com. Enter **Venezia Santa Lucia** for the station in Venice and **Padova** for Padua.

By car: take the A4 autostrada highway that connects Venice with Milan, Padua is at 41 km from Venice. The autostrada A13 to Bologna starts south of town in Padua.

Brenta's Riviera Villas

The Brenta Riviera is made up of districts and green spots along the ancient course of a river linking Padua to Venice. This was the ideal extension of Venice onto the mainland, almost a continuation of the lagoon city: between the 16th and 18th centuries the Brenta Riviera experienced a golden age which turned it into a privileged holiday resort for rich Venetian nobles.

They built dozens and dozens of villas along its riverbanks, designed and decorated by masters of Italian art, visited by artists, popes, kings and men of culture, envied for their beauty, inhabited as country seats where they celebrated with ritual floating processions, sumptuous dinners and festivities lasting until dawn. Buildings of the villas along the Riviera began in the 15th century, when Venice extended its dominion over the mainland.

Already by the 16th century, there were gems such as villa Foscari at Malcontenta, designed by Palladio, or villa Soranzo at Fiesso with its outside frescoed by Paolo Veronese's brother. In the subsequent century, the flights steps down onto the water's edge increased, gardens were peopled with busts and baroque decorations such as in villa Morosini in Mirano and villa Sagredo in Vigonovo.

Villa Foscari at the Malcontenta in Mira

In the 18th century these spaces were expanded through ingenious perspectives creating triumphs such as villa Widmann at Mira Porte and villa Pisani at Stra, a genuine Doge's palace on dry land.Lovers of Italian art forms can find an infinite number of attractions on the Brenta Riviera. The architecture of the villas is remarkable for the variety of styles which go from the 16th-century austerity to the unleashed fantasies of the 17th century, then on to the rational style of the 18th century. It is also worth recalling the churches with their wealth of precious paintings and the simple but interesting examples of lesser architecture. Inside the villas there are whole cycles of paintings.

From March to October, the stately homes are best admired from the water's edge; the opportunity is provided by the Burchiello, the legendary boat mentioned by Goldoni which daily links Padua to Venice, stopping off to enable visits to the most beautiful villas on the Riviera.

I Battelli del Brenta

The passenger boat operator " I Battelli del Brenta" (The boats of the Brenta Canal) provide enjoyable guided public cruises, from Venice to Padua or vice-versa, along the Brenta Canal (Riviera del Brenta), visiting some of the Venetian Villas, summer residences of the 16th century, with stops at the monumental palaces with its legendary frescoes.

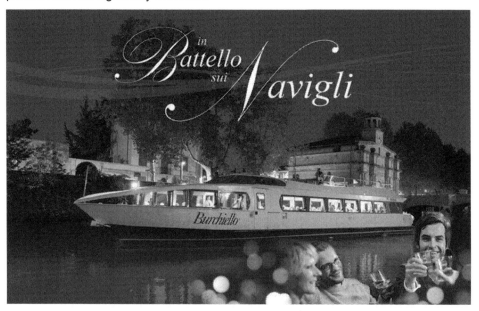

Once along this waterway sailed the "burchielli", boats that carried the Venetian nobleman; nowadays all the boats that cruise along the Brenta Canal are called "burchielli".

The company "I Battelli del Brenta" has many boats carrying from 70 to 135 passengers and romantic "Burci", restored wooden old barges.

Food and Wine of the Brenta Riviera

Brenta Riviera cuisine is a feature of International gastronomical guide books for the professional talent acquired in preparing fish. Lying behind the Venetian lagoon and the "white fish" breading areas of the river deltas, Brenta gastronomy is the heir of a refined tradition which has succeeded in conjugating antique local recipes with a centuries-old experience of the nobles cuisine.

There are hot and cold hors d'oeuvres for the most refined of palates, first courses born from the happy combination of aromatic herbs and peak quality fish, mixed fries and grills which simply emphasize the absolute freshness of the products.

Veneto: the festivals

Marostica: partita a scacchi di Margherita Forni

Partita a Scacchi (Marostica)

Every even year, in September, a game of chess using live pieces is played. The tradition was started in 1454 when two noblemen, Renaldo D'Anganaro and Vieri da Vallanora fell in love with the beautiful Lionora, daughter of the local lord, Taddeo Parisio. As was the custom at that time, they challenged each other to a duel to win the hand of Lionora. The Lord of Marostica, not wanting to make an enemy of either suitor or lose them in a duel, forbade the encounter.

Instead he decreed that the two rivals would play a chess game, and the winner would have the hand of Lionora. The loser of the chess game would also join the family, through marrying Oldrada. The game took place on the square in front of the Lower Castle with supporters carrying the noble ensigns of Whites and Blacks, in the presence of the Lord, his noble daughter, the Lords of Angarano and Vallonara, the court and the entire town population.

The Lord also decided the challenge would be honoured by an exhibition of armed men, foot-soldiers and knights, with fireworks and dances and music. This event is now faithfully reenacted on the square of Marostica every second Friday, Saturday and Sunday of September of "even" years. The orders are still given to the cast today in the dialect of the "Serenissima Republic of Venezia".

Concerti in Villa (Vicenza)

The Veneto region around Vicenza opens up its villas or their grounds for a series of summertime concerts and performances. From famous masterpieces like Palladio's La Rotonda to little-known Renaissance villas, the settings are memorable and the music is sweet. June and July.

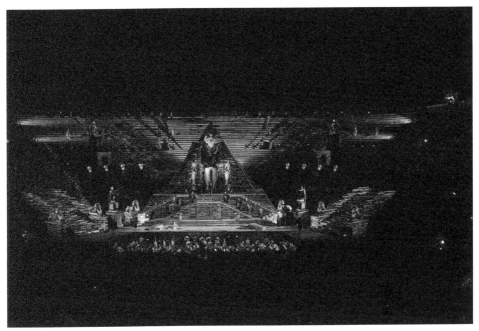

Aida in Verona

Opera in Arena (Verona)

La Scala in Milan and La Fenice in Venice may be more famous, but few opera stages in Italy have a more natural dramatic setting than Verona's ancient Roman amphitheater.

Every season they put on *Aida* as they have since 1913, surrounded by other operatic masterpieces by Giuseppe Verdi.

For a huge 2,000-year-old sports stadium open to the sky, the Arena enjoys surprisingly good acoustics. Late June through August.

Festival Shakespeariano (Verona)

Verona mixes its two powerhouse attractions — ancient Roman heritage and Shakespearean fame — in a theater festival of Shakespeare's plays (along with ballets and concerts, from classical to jazz) put on in the garden-set ruins of the Teatro Romano ancient theater. Since 1998, they've invited the Royal Shakespeare Company to come and perform (naturally) *Romeo and Juliet* and *Two Gentlemen of Verona*, as well as other plays, in English.

Veneto Food and Recipes

In Veneto there are many kind of Salami, a lot of local regional Recipes, they pair very well with the local Wine. It's all part of the best Italian Food.

The 'Veneto' is an essentially agricultural region growing wheat, maize, mulberry bushes, olive, fruit trees and vines. The industrial sector includes oil refineries, smelting works and chemical plants which are concentrated in the vicinity of *Venice* at *Mestre-Marghera*, as well as a large production of hydro-electric energy in the valleys of the Pre-Alps. The latter supplies the textile industry.

The landscape is punctuated by two small volcanic groups, the *Berici* Mountains south of *Vicenza* and the *Euganean Hills* near *Padua*. The slopes of these blackish heights carry vines, peach orchards and are the site of hot springs.

In the Po delta (*Polesine*) and that of the *Adige* lie impoverished, grandiose and desolate areas, subject to river floods. Following reclamation certain areas are farmed on an industrial scale for wheat and sugar beet.

The coastline takes the form of lagoons (*lido*) separated from the sea by spits of sand pierced by gaps (*porti*). *Venice*, whose industrial sector is continually growing, is built on piles in one of these lagoons.

Veneto food: as in the Po Plain, the people eat *polenta*, a form of semolina made from maize, sometimes accompanied by little birds, *risi e bisi* (rice and peas), and *fegato alla veneziana* (calf's liver fried with onions). The shell-fish, eels and dried cod (baccala) are excellent. The best wines come from the district of Verona; Valpolicella and Bardolino, rose' or red, perfumed and slightly sparkling, and Soave, which is white and strong.

Venetian cuisine is known for its variety of dishes and ingredients. This can be expected in a lagoon city which, though born of its own waters, has always maintained close ties with the mainland as well as flourishing trade routes with many faraway countries, from northern Europe to the far East.

Here you find not only the dried Baltic cod and the exquisite Asian spices, but also the genuine if perhaps more modest fresh vegetables from the estuary islands, fish from the Venice lagoon and game fowl captured in the barene, or shallows. A visit to Venice offers an opportunity to discover a fascinating gastronomic tradition.

Venetian cuisine is simple and tasty, fish-based. Vongole, Capparozzoli, Cappe (clams), Cozze (mussels), Gamberi, Gamberetti, Gamberoni, Scampi, Astici (all in the family of shrimps), Seppie, Seppioline (cuttle-fish) are the most popular. It is, however, difficult if not impossible to have fresh fish on Mondays because most fishermen do not work on Sunday nights. You will also notice there is no fresh fish at the market or in the shops just frozen.

Grappa

Grappa is grape pomace, the remnants of winegrape pressings. Derived from the crushed skins, pulp and seeds of winegrapes, grappa is produced throughout Italy and is generally considered to be one of the most elementary of distilled spirits-an authentic case of Distilling 101, if you will. Regardless of which accounts of the history of distilling you adhere to, it is certain that distillation of some forms of grape juice was occurring in Italy by the 12th century. For centuries, grappa has been the peasant's drink of choice. Farmers in bucolic districts such as Piedmont, the Veneto, Umbria, Friuli, and Tuscany customarily wanted a strong drink to help patch up their workday wounds and salve their aches for the night It was grappa that became Italy's national spirit. It is a liqueur now.

Specialty Foods of Veneto

Risi, or rice, is a mainstay on the Venetian menu, but it's generally served differently than in most other areas of Italy. Rice is never eaten by itself, but always cooked and served with other ingredients, such as lamb, sausages, chicken livers, tripe, beans, and raisins, as well as with fish and shellfish. The most famous Venetian rice dishes are *risi e bisi* (rice and fresh peas) and *risi e figadini* (rice with chicken livers), which have the consistency of a thick soup. Risotto – made with fish, beans, chicken, veal, or vegetables such as fennel or zucchini – is also popular in the Veneto, with specialties such as **Risotto alla sbirraglia:** spring chicken and lean veal braised with rice and vegetables and **Risotto primavera:** diced string beans, artichokes, tomatoes, carrots and potatoes united with peas and asparagus tips and braised with rice in the spring.

Another specialty Veneto food is *Baccala'*, dried, salted cod fish, is one food that the people of Venice and the larger region of Veneto agree on. It is widely served throughout the area, at gala dinners or on everyday tables, often mixed with polenta into a delicate, delicious "cream" that is eaten as an appetizer with cocktails or as a first course. *Baccala' alla Visentina*, which is a version of *baccala'* that hails from the city of Vicenza, is a slow-cooking dish with many variations, and which ingredients should or should not be included (milk, celery, potatoes) is often the subject of heated but friendly debate among Venetian food lovers.

Polenta, a modest dish made from cornmeal, is a staple food of much of Northern Italy, but nowhere is it more popular than in the Veneto region. It was (and still is) traditionally prepared by stirring cornmeal, water, and salt over heat constantly for 40 to 45 minutes with a wooden stirring stick called a *mescola*. (To ease the burden, families would often take "shifts" as stirrers.) The resulting "mush" is then poured onto a wooden board to cool, and cut with kitchen string while still hot (a knife can be used once the polenta is set). Today, automatic stirring machines make the job easier, but they do not supply the togetherness of sitting around the kitchen and stirring the fragrant polenta as it cooks. **Pasticcio di polenta:** layers of fried polenta and stew of wood pigeon with mushrooms baked in pie crust.

Veneto's food contribution to Italy's pasta culture is a style of fresh pasta called *bigoli*, which gets its name from the traditional kitchen implement that's used to make it, called a *bigolaro*, a four-inch-wide bronze tube. *Bigoli*, a long, spaghetti-style pasta with a hole in its middle, is made on a hand-operated press by forcing pasta dough through the **bigolaro**, then cutting the strands to the desired length. A typical Venetian preparation is *bigoli in salsa*, which tosses the*bigoli* with a delicious sauce of anchovies, olive oil, and cooked onions and **bigoli co l'anara:**"spaghetti" and sauce of duck liver and innards with vegetables and herbs.

Veneto Recipes

Veneto typical food:
Pasticcio di polenta: layers of fried polenta and stew of wood pigeon with mushrooms baked in pie crust.
Pastissada de caval: horse meat stewed with tomatoes, onions and herbs in red wine.

Veneto Recipes:
Baccala mantecato – Dried Cod
Bigoli co l'anara – "spaghetti" and sauce of duck liver and innards with vegetables and herbs.
Capesante in tecia – Scallops in Tecia
Carpaccio – the original (named for the Venetian Renaissance painter) was thin-sliced raw beef dressed with mayonnaise containing mustard and Worcestershire sauce, though popularity has inspired creations with meat, fish, cheese, mushrooms and truffles.
Fagioli alla Veneta – Beans and Anchovies
Fegato alla veneziana – Calf's liver sauteed with onions, parsley and sage in

butter and oil with a hint of vinegar.

Fettuccine Alfredo

Granseola alla veneziana – The meat of boiled spider crab pounded in a mortar and served in the hollowed shell with olive oil, pepper, lemon, parsley.

Pasta e fasioi – Noodles of any type and beans in a thick minestra, often flavored with onion, carrot, celery, pork rind, though recipes vary around the region.

Prosciutto di San Daniele Recipes

Risi e bisi – Rice and peas

Risotto alla sbirraglia – spring chicken and lean veal braised with rice and vegetables.

Risotto primavera – diced string beans, artichokes, tomatoes, carrots and potatoes united with peas and asparagus tips and braised with rice in the spring.

Salsa peverada – Spicy Sauce

Sarde in saor – Marinated sardines

Sardelle in saor – Sardines in Saor

Savor di frutta – Fruit Spice

Sopa coada – Squab Soup

Tiramisu – Coffee-flavored cream of mascarpone and eggs, layered with savoiardi (ladyfingers) and topped with curls of bitter chocolate.

Torresani allo spiedo - pigeons roasted on the spit with salt pork basted with oil containing mashed bay leaf, rosemary, juniper berries.

Things to Know

Italy Entry Requirements

Travelers from other countries in the European Union do not need a visa when visiting Italy by virtue of the Schengen agreement. Additionally Swiss travelers are also exempt. Visitors from certain other countries such as the USA, Canada, Japan, Israel, Australia, Brazil and New Zealand do not need visas if their stay in Italy does not exceed 90 days. When entering Italy you will be required to make a declaration of presence, either at the airport, or at a police station within eight days of arrival. This applies to visitors from other Schengen countries, as well as those visiting from non-Schengen countries.

Health Insurance in Italy

Citizens of EU countries are covered for emergency health care in Italy. UK residents, as well as visitors from Switzerland are covered by the European Health Insurance Card (EHIC), which can be applied for free of charge. Visitors from non-Schengen countries will need to show proof of private health insurance that is valid for the duration of their stay in Italy (that offers at least € 37,500 coverage), as part of their visa application. No special vaccinations are required.

Traveling with Pets in Italy

Italy participates in the Pet Travel Scheme (PETS) which allows UK residents to travel with their pets without requiring quarantine upon re-entry. Certain conditions need to be met. The animal must be microchipped and up to date on rabies vaccinations. In the case of dogs, a vaccination against canine distemper is also required by the Italian authorities. When traveling from the USA, your pet will need to be micro-chipped or marked with an identifying tattoo and up to date on rabies vaccinations. An EU Annex IV Veterinary Certificate for Italy will need to be issued by an accredited veterinarian. On arrival in Italy, you can apply for an EU pet passport to ease your travel in other EU countries.

Currency in Italy

Italy's currency is the Euro, issued in notes in denominations of € 500, € 200, € 100, € 50, € 20, € 10 and € 5. Coins are issued in denominations of € 2, € 1, 50c, 20c, 10c, 5c, 2c and 1c.

Banking & ATMs in Italy

Using ATMs, called Bancomats,in Italy, to withdraw money is simple if your ATM card is compatible with the MasterCard/ Cirrus or Visa/ Plus networks. There is a € 250 limit on daily withdrawals. Italian machines are configured for 4-digit PIN numbers, although some machines will be able to handle longer PIN numbers. Bear in mind some Bancomats can run out of cash over weekends and that the more remote villages may not have adequate banking facilities so plan ahead.

Credit Cards

Credit cards are accepted in most Italian businesses. While Visa and MasterCard are accepted universally, most tourist oriented businesses also accept American Express and Diners Club. Credit cards must be fitted with a microchip that require a PIN for each transaction. A few ticket machines, self-service vendors and other businesses may not be configured to accept the older magnetic strip credit cards.

Tourist Taxes in Italy

Tourist tax varies from city to city, as each municipality sets its own rate. The money is collected by your accommodation and depends on the standard of accommodation, with a five star establishment levying a higher amount than a four star or three star establishment. You can expect to pay somewhere between € 1 and € 7 per night, in popular destinations like Rome, Venice, Milan and Florence. In some regions, the rate is also adjusted seasonally. Children are usually exempt until at least the age of 10 and sometimes up to the age of 18. In certain areas, disabled persons and their companions also qualify for discounted rates. Tourist tax is payable directly to the hotel or guesthouse before the end of your stay.

Reclaiming Italian IVA (VAT)

If you are from outside the European Union, you can claim back VAT (Value Added Tax), called IVA in Italy, paid on your purchases in Italy. The VAT rate in Italy is 20 percent and this can be claimed back on your purchases if certain conditions are met. The refund applies for purchases over € 155 in a single store. The merchant needs to be partnered with a VAT refund program. This will be indicated if the shop displays a "Tax Free" sign. The shop assistant will fill out a form for reclaiming VAT. When you submit this at the airport, you will receive your refund.

Tipping Policy in Italy

Your bill usually includes the phrase "coperto e servizio", that means that a service charge is already included. Most waiting staff in Italy are salaried workers, but if the service is excellent, a few euros extra will be appreciated.

Mobile Phones

Most EU countries, including Italy use the GSM mobile service. This means that most UK phones and some US and Canadian phones and mobile devices will work in Italy. While you could check with your service provider about coverage before you leave, using your own service in roaming mode involves additional costs. The alternative is to purchase an Italian SIM card to use during your stay in Italy, this will work if your phone is unlocked.

Dialing Code

The international dialing code for Italy is + 39.

Emergency Numbers

Police: 113
Fire: 115
Ambulance: 118
MasterCard: 800 789 525
Visa: 800 819 014

Electricity

Electricity: 220 volts Frequency: 50 Hz Italian electricity sockets are compatible with the Type L plugs, a plug that features three round pins or prongs, arranged in a straight line. An alternate is the two-pronged Type C Euro adaptor. If traveling from the USA, you will need a power converter or transformer to convert the voltage from 220 to 110, to avoid damage to your appliances. The latest models of many laptops, camcorders, mobile phones and digital cameras are dual-voltage with a built in converter.

Italian Drinking Laws

The legal drinking age in Italy is 16. While drinking in public spaces is allowed, public drunkenness is not tolerated. Alcohol is sold in bars, wine shops, liquor stores and grocery shops.

Italian Smoking Laws

In 2005, Italy implemented a policy banning smoking from public places such as bars, restaurants, nightclubs and working places, limiting it to specially designated smoking rooms.

Italian Driving Laws

The Italians drive on the right hand side of the road. A driver's license from any of the European Union member countries is valid in Italy. Visitors from non-EU countries will require an International Driving Permit that must remain current throughout the duration of their stay in Italy.

The speed limit on Italy's autostrade is 130km per hour and 110km per hour on main extra-urban roads, but this is reduced by 20km to 110km and 90km respectively in rainy weather. On secondary extra-urban roads, the speed limit is 90km per hour; on urban highways, it is 70km per hour and on urban roads, the speed limit is 50km per hour.

You are not allowed to drive in the ZTL or Limited Traffic Zone (or zona traffico limitato in Italian) unless you have a special permit.

Visitors to Italy are allowed to drive their own non-Italian vehicles in the country for a period of up to six months. After this, they will be required to obtain Italian registration with Italian license plates.

Italy has very strict laws against driving under the influence of alcohol. The blood alcohol limit is 0.05 and drivers caught above the limit face penalties such as fines of up to € 6000, confiscation of their vehicles, suspension of their licenses and imprisonment

Restaurant basics

The standard procedures of a restaurant meal throughout Italy are different from those in the United States (and most other places). When you sit down in a ristorante, you're expected to order two courses at a minimum, such as a primo (first course) and a secondo (second course), or an antipasto (starter) followed by a primo or secondo, or a secondo with dessert. Traditionally, a secondo is not a "main course" that would serve as a full meal. The crucial rule of restaurant dining is that you should order at least two courses. It's a common mistake for tourists to order only a secondo, thinking they're getting a "main course" complete with side dishes. What they wind up with is one lonely piece of meat. Eateries are quite used to diners who order courses to split; but, if you're not so hungry, you might head for a pizzeria or bacaro to sample some quick bites.

Hotel Basics

Hotels in Italy are usually well maintained (especially if they've earned our recommendation in this book), but in some respects they won't match what you find at comparably priced U.S. lodgings.

Keep the following points in mind as you set your expectations, and you're likely to have a good experience: Rooms are usually smaller, particularly in cities. If you're truly cramped, ask for another room, but don't expect things to be spacious. A "double bed" is commonly two singles pushed together. In the bathroom, tubs are not a given— request one if it's essential. In budget places, showers sometimes use a drain in the middle of the bathroom floor. Washcloths are a rarity. Most hotels have satellite TV, but there are fewer channels than in the United States, and only one or two will be in English. Don't expect wall-to-wall carpeting; tile floors are the norm.

What to pack

In summer stick with light clothing, but toss in a sweater in case of cool evenings, especially if you're headed for the islands. Sunglasses, a hat, and sunblock are essential. In winter, bring a coat, gloves, hat, and scarf. Winter weather is milder than in the northern and central United States, but central heating isn't always reliable. Bring comfortable walking shoes in any season. As a rule, Italians dress well. Men aren't required to wear ties or jackets anywhere except in the most formal restaurants, but are expected to look reasonably sharp — and they do. A certain modesty (no bare shoulders or knees) is expected in churches, and strictly enforced in many.

Other tourist guides

All tourist guides from Enrico Massetti are listed on his web site at http://enricomassetti.com/tourist-e-guides/ and can be purchased in printed form as well as in all digital formats at all major online stores.

The Author

Enrico Massetti was born in Milano. Now he lives in Washington DC, USA, but he regularly visits his hometown, and enjoys going around all the places near his home town that can be reached by public transportation.

Enrico can be reached at enricomassetti@msn.com.

Made in the USA
Monee, IL
24 May 2022

96952646R00052